EVERYTHING YOU ALWAYS WANTED TO KNOW ABOUT BUSINESS WRITING

*BUT NEVER LEARNED IN SCHOOL!

Dr. William Russo

About the Author

Author of works on Hollywood history and sports, including *Great Sports Stories: The Legendary Films, The Next James Dean* and *Audie Murphy, Vietnam, and the Making of The Quiet American*, Dr. William Russo taught for many years at Curry College in Milton, Massachusetts, creating the successful course on Business Writing that served hundreds of students. He holds his doctorate from the University of Massachusetts with a focus on literacy and language arts. Dr. Russo also served as a film contributor for *Big Reel*. He has collaborated with Emmy-winning writer and film star Jan Merlin on *The Paid Companion of J. Wilkes Booth, Troubles in a Golden Eye, Hanging with Billy Budd*, and *MGM Makes Boys Town*, and has edited a variety of fiction and nonfiction works on topics such as Multiple Sclerosis and the Vietnamese Boat People as Chief Editor of Lukeion Press. His recent books include *Riding James Kirkwood's Pony* and *Sex, Drugs, Sports, & Whimsy*.

STRATEGIES for a variety of problems or occasions listed in this booklet can be adapted for both letter and memorandum format, for e-mail or blog, newsletter or speech. Explained in this booklet are templates of action.

These segments are:

Tweets.
Abstract Writing.
Aperçu.
Literary Digest.
Producing Minutes.
Conspectus.
Routine Inquiry.
Panegyric.
Complaint/Claims Letter.
Thank You Letter.
Invitation Letter.
Cover Letter.
Resume Rules.
Sales Letter.
Bad News Letter.
Short Memorandum Report.
Personnel Report.
Addressing an Envelope.

An INTRODUCTION

Business writing is a science. It is also a hostile act, but most instructors of writing teach it as an art. This may account for the trouble many students encounter during their education with the process of writing critical essays or research papers.

To suggest that business writing is an art conveys an aura of mystical divination, inspiration, and innate talent.

The process of writing is a practical and necessary task, perhaps even a legal one. As such, the rules of writing can be codified scientifically.

My purpose in this concise and condensed booklet is to provide the reader with a few guidelines for writing. There is nothing mystical, intuitive, or amazing about this process. The rules are universal formulas for success, as scientific as physics or psychology. Experts call this transactional writing because need requires the writer transact business with his audience.

You can use these templates and strategies in a small business you run, or in your daily life. Transactional writing happens when you apply for a job, or file a complaint, or deliver bad news.

These strategies can be used orally (if you sell cars or sell ideas) or in writing, if you want to persuade people to follow a candidate for political office.

This guidebook for transactional writing gives a few pre-writing ideas.

Some rules will seem superficial; some may feel condescending. The hope is that you will see a new perspective on old rules that you may not have consciously considered in many years.

Syntax, semantics, and structure, can be fresh if viewed on their most basic level. With a few tactics on visual and verbal cues of learning, this booklet may give a formula, not precise, but standard, on how to produce professional reports. Of course, inevitably, you are the one to adopt or to ignore these suggestions. Their incorporation into your writing will improve the style of your all-important project.

In order to understand and practice these rules, the reader and potential writer must know the definitions of several terms that explain the process.

These concepts are the framework on which all of the writing strategies to follow will be built. The business writer should know, however, that creativity and sharp thinking are individualistic. The proper diction, the element of diplomatic phrasing, and the use of logic in analysis, are all beyond the boundary of this booklet. These skills can also be learned and improved.

What we seek to do here is provide a short and direct approach to business writing.

Writing, like any other science, must be studied intensively and practiced often in order to be truly effective in its application or its cognitive transformation of business communication.

Dr. William Russo

OUTLINING and WRITING

AUDIENCE:
You must know for whom you are writing. This may seem rather obvious. It is not always. To send the memorandum to the wrong person could have dire consequences for you. Always respect the chain of command and follow proper channels for all letters and memoranda. Your audience has a demographic identity: education, cultural background, predilections, and its particular language skills. You must write to suit that person or group.

PURPOSE:
This too may seem obvious. However, there are hundreds of reasons to write, each with a fine difference from another point. To lose sight of the purpose will cause you to fail to do what you intend.

FORM:
Two public forms of writing exist. One is formal; that is objective, detached, not using first-person pronouns, or addressing the reader as you. Directives and reports are formal.

The second form is general. This is the form of most memoranda and letters; it is personal without being formal. You can use "I" or "we". The reader is called "you"; however, do not use slang or clichés.

THESIS:
Every piece of business writing has a thesis. It is the first sentence of your writing, no matter what the point. A thesis is one sentence generalization that tells the reader your main idea, your purpose, your tone, and other subtle factors. A thesis can also be called a hook in persuasion, being more brazen and lively.

INTRODUCTION:

Every piece of writing has an introductory paragraph. The introduction is comprised of the thesis and topic ideas. Your introduction gives the reader a sense of what you are writing.

DEDUCTION:

This is a style of logic. Deduction in paragraphing is the use of a direct approach. You confront the reader the with paragraph point as the start--and follow with the specifics of your case. Deduction starts with the general and works toward the minute; it starts with abstraction and gives concrete example.

INDUCTION:

This style of logic in paragraphing is subtle and is used in persuasion and bad news often. Opinions often cause emotional reactions. Induction uses specifics and detail to lead the reader to accept an opinion he might otherwise reject. With induction you write from the concrete to the abstract, or from the specific to the general.

TOPIC SENTENCE.

Just as every piece of writing has a thesis, every paragraph has a topic sentence. That is a short, general opinion about the subject at hand. When a topic sentence appears at the start of a paragraph that is called deductive. When it appears at the end of a paragraph, style is called inductive.

DETAILS.

These are the specifics that are the basis for your paragraphs. Details are concrete examples to prove the validity of your topic sentence. One detail does not prove a generalization. A good paragraph has many details.

TRANSITIONS:

These are words or phrases that start a sentence or a paragraph. These are usually conversational expressions that give your writing a more pleasant or stylish sound. Transitions can also be used to overcome writer's block by helping you start the next sentence in your letter or memo.

GOOD WRITING HABITS

PREPARATION.

Start with an analysis of the question posed and of your commitment to answer it. What point of view will enable you to both teach the reader and learn something about your writing? Think through the scope, scale, and style to set the boundaries of your essay, and to make learning possible.

TIMETABLE.

Set aside a third or a half of writing time for preparation and planning -- to think through the subject, and your approach to answering the question. As part of planning, generate your provisional thesis and because-clauses. By the end of your planning, you should have an outline of your whole argument. You can use the remaining half of your allotted time for two complete revisions, feedback, and then proofreading.

STRUCTURAL PLAN.

Before you write, think of the final draft as a coherent, unified essay with a beginning that states the question and your answer, as well as invites the reader in; a middle that meets the other side of your argument head-on, and then provides evidence for your own in the order of increasing importance; and an end that not only summarizes but states for the reader the new perspective your answer gives on the original question.

PROVISIONAL THESIS.

Take a stand on the question, and commit yourself to an answer, with evidence and examples. This provisional thesis will become more elaborate as the project unfolds, but it starts you on the way toward discovering and presenting meaning to your reader.

BECAUSE-CLAUSES.

This spontaneous list of "reasons" for your provisional thesis will provide you with some of the language for your final draft, but more than that, it gives you the raw material for deciding what you want to say, and what you can leave out. It is the basis for your raw draft. Some clauses run on for a paragraph or a page or two. These rough ideas and examples reflect your commitment to the subject. Test each clause to see if it is true or useful in your argument. If you can think of opposing arguments, so can your reader. If you meet them head-on before presenting your own argument, you gain the reader's trust.

Also include the other side in your provisional thesis. A good pattern for your thesis/introduction is: "Although_____, it is better to_____, because_____."

ARGUMENT-OUTLINE.
Once you've analyzed the because-clauses, and selected your raw material, make a quick outline of your argument to establish coherence among your ideas. Put your most convincing point last in the middle section, where it will naturally lead to the conclusion. If you group ideas under headings in your outline you will have the essence of transitions from one section to the next. Selecting and ordering the best of the raw material enables you to adapt your provisional thesis to the sense and sequence of your argument.

RAW DRAFT.
Fit the blocks of selected material from your because-clauses into your outline to produce a raw draft. Then, read through for coherence, cutting repetitions, inconsistencies, and any tangential or too abstract material. Seek some feedback. The questions will elicit answers from the writer that should be part of the writing in the first place.

SECOND READING.
First cuts give coherence. Your second reading ensures that every example, every piece of evidence, every sentence, every word contributes to the overall unity of your essay.

STANDARD OPERATING PROCEDURE

APPEARANCE.
You should take some pride in your personal work. Be sure there are no heading inconsistencies with underlining or italics or silly diction mistakes on your work. Cognitive control of content has its psychological values.

ADEQUATE CONTENT.
Be sure that you have the sufficient number of paragraphs to make your strategy work effectively. Be certain that you cite adequate detail, spaced in its own sentence. Don't attempt to cram all of your details into one sentence. Give the reader time to digest each example.

INTRODUCTION.
The first paragraph of every piece of business writing should have a thesis.

BODY PARAGRAPHS.
Check to be certain that inductive paragraphs have topic sentences at the end; deductive should have topic sentences at the start. Some memoranda have topic headings; letters do not.

SPELLING AND PUNCTUATION.
Have a dictionary, thesaurus, and grammar book by your side. Check anything of which you are uncertain.

FORMAT.
Have you placed colons after the greeting of letters? Are there commas after each closing? Are headings consistent--all caps are all underscored?

TRANSITIONS.
Is there a logical sequence to the order of your detail? Commas are after all transitional words or expressions that start sentences?

RUN-ON SENTENCES, COMMA SPLICE SENTENCES, AND FRAGMENTS.
Nothing is more mortifying than a grievous grammatical flaw. Proofread each sentence from last to first, as units, examining all with a critical eye for overall content.

DICTION.
The key to successful writing is in your verbs. Select strong, expressive verbs. Avoid clichés--or from using the verb 'get' or 'got' or 'gotten.'

TRANSITIONS

TO ADD:
Again,
And,
Thereafter,
And then,
Soon,
Besides,
Afterward,
Equally important,
Then,
Finally,
Later,
Further,
Furthermore,
Moreover,
Too,
Next,
Last,

TO COMPARE OR TO CONTRAST:
On the contrary,
However,
After all,
Yet,
For all that,
Still,
In contrast,
Nevertheless,
At the same time,
Nonetheless,
While this is true,
Notwithstanding,
Meanwhile,
On the other hand,

TO GIVE EXAMPLES or TO EMPHASIZE:

For instance,
Obviously,
For example,
In fact,
To demonstrate,
Indeed,
To illustrate,
In any case,
As a matter of fact,
In point of fact,

TO SUMMARIZE:

In short,
On the whole,
In other words,
In conclusion,

TO CONCLUDE:
Therefore,
Accordingly,
Thus,
As a result,
Consequently,
As a consequence,

Rules of Etiquette in Business Writing and in Online Communication

E-mail is a valuable tool for reaching people around the business world, sending quick updates, or exchanging ideas. The Internet is an instant roundtable. "As we proceed more and more with online networking, the people who stand out will know how to combine the human skills with the technical skills," states Susan RoAne, author of *How to Work a Room*.

One of the best things about online class is that e-mails and chat comments can be sent and reviewed when it is convenient for both the sender and the receiver. During discussions online, the same rules apply.

Acceptable Behaviors

1. Be appropriately businesslike. Be civil in your e-mail as you would in a face-to-face meeting. Recently a superintendent of schools in Massachusetts put something disparaging about students on Facebook for her friends, but pushed the wrong button. All the city students saw her snide comments.

2. Make sure to think before you write a comment.

3. Stay on-task. You should not change the topic or answer a different question, though you may ask for a clarification on the topic at hand.

4. Allow others to respond and react.

5. Proofread for typos, including grammatical errors and misspelling. Use lower and uppercase letters. (Typing in all-caps is considered SHOUTING.)
6. Acknowledge e-mails within a day, at latest, as a courtesy.

7. Beware of sexual innuendo. You do not want to risk offending people. You surely do not want to jeopardize your career; people have been dismissed for sending suggestive or offensive e-mail.

8. Resist the impulse to forward jokes, cartoons, or other diversions.

9. Remember e-mail doesn't allow you to use body language and vocal inflections. Your words are all you have.

10. Avoid emoticons or text message abbreviations. This course practices good writing and standard communication skills. You already know how to do it incorrectly, and now you want to learn how to do it properly.

TWEETS

Twitter accounts now proliferate. People on Twitter can amass a following of thousands of social connections in their network. Many do not realize that the site is not a frivolous place to mention ideas or random thoughts: it is a major public statement. You are putting yourself in a spotlight.

Twitter's tweets are the ultimate in business writing. You are presenting yourself to the world and using the most public forum of business presentation: your own words. A quick examination of typical tweets will be a mess of misspellings, variant abbreviations, and slang, that is outright embarrassing to the sender, though they'd hardly understand that, feeling the tweet is merely a personal expression. Unlike texting, which goes to a specific and private audience, a tweet goes to anyone who wants to read it.

Your tweet is 140 characters, by the rules of Twitter. Let's put that into clearer terms. A tweet is about the length of a good college-level complex sentence of twenty to twenty-five words. You can make shorter sentences and attach a URL for sending your follower to another site for more details. This is an extraordinary opportunity to present your public self. As far as public image is concerned, your tweets may be the most damning factor in your career and life. Tweets can inform, inflame, and insult.

If you want an example of superior tweets, you need only go to Dame Elizabeth Taylor, a legendary movie star, whose tweets are clear, concise, precise, grammatical, and the epitome of the brilliant sound byte. Employers and consumers may take a look at your tweets and your social network page to gain a better sense of your identity.

Based on typical tweets, the average user has become damaged goods. For many out there, you have just lost the job, the customer, the lifetime partner, and perhaps your money.

Tweet like your life depended on it. It does.

TEN COMMON MISTAKES ON LETTER FORMAT

1. Date is always centered under stationery name: a comma between date and year.

2. Audience's address has comma between city and state; none between zip and state.

3. Dear is always on the margin; use a name or title ALWAYS. In business, greetings end with a COLON, not a comma. Commas are strictly for personal correspondence greetings.

4. Conservatives indent; liberals use block form. Take the cue from your supervisor. It is correct to indent.

5. You double-space (skip a line) between paragraphs in letters and memoranda.

6. You single-space the lines of all paragraphs.

7. The first word only of the close is in caps; follow close with a comma.

8. You sign between close and your typed name.

9. Post scripts are not encouraged: if you use one, "P.S." is followed by a comma or colon.

10. Enc. means enclosure(s); c.c. abbreviates copies are going to people listed. p.c. means photocopy.

FIVE COMMON MISTAKES OF MEMO FORMAT

1. The word "MEMORANDUM" is usually typed at the top of the page (in caps), but not in e-mail.

2. The four directional headings are all in caps.

3. You do not "sign" a memo; you put your initials after your typed name at the top.

4. The subject line should be followed by a short phrase, not a sentence, with individual words' first letters in caps.

5. After the body, you do not sign with a close. That technique is strictly for letters. You sign your initials where indicated.

NOTICE

In the following prescriptive memo and letter formats, each segment has a heading.

These are NOT included in your actual letters + memoranda. These are STRICTLY for directions for you.

PANDECT OR LIST

One popular technique in business lately is the pandect. In essence, this device puts information into a list format. Often, the list is a code of rules, regulations, suggestions, or improvements. The strategy can be used for humor.

There are two kinds of pandect lists: ascending order, starting with the least important and moving to the top-most item. Descending order is the reverse: it begins with the most important item and works down to the least in priority. Descending order is also used in chronology, from start to finish. It is more often the technique of written lists. Lists require a proper format of grammar and structure for readability and coherence. Layout is highly important. The thesis sentence heads the list and introduces the concept about to be presented. An opening sentence ends with a colon:

1. Body of the list can be numbered, lettered, or bulleted;

2. Listings are indented;

3. List items should be double-spaced for readability;

4. Punctuation used must be consistent, usually semi-colons;

5. Items must be all of similar construction: all commands, all complete sentences (as here), or all fragments (least favored);
6. Second lines are indented too, as above;

7. First letters of each item should be capitalized for emphasis;

8. Lists usually have significant or magical numbers (Top Ten, Seven Deadly Sins, Ten Commandment);

9. Final list items end with a period;

10. Ends of lists need to be followed by a summary statement.

Good writers know the rules of pandects and use them to enhance the readability and effectiveness of their writing.

ABSTRACT WRITING

Abstracts are summary accounts, in long narrative paragraph format. These are almost always used for condensing scientific writing to a bite-size for reading. This form is not recommended to summarize novels, plots, plays, or stories. It is most frequently an issue of long reports, making the document more quickly digested. Indeed, some call this style a digest.

An abstract is essentially a brief explanation or recapitulation of a document. Abstracts give an accurate sense of a document without any editorial opinion on the content. In this the abstract is truly a work of journalism. Abstracts are formal and maintain, as much as possible the style and form of the original, to give the reader a true sense of the complete report and its diction. Abstracts can be up to three paragraphs in length, but seldom are more than 200 words.

As a long paragraph, the abstract does not always follow the rules of tradition paragraphing. There are several key facts that MUST be present in an abstract.

In a sentence or two, you must state the THESIS OF THE ORIGINAL DOCUMENT.

Next, you must identify the author or researcher and his credentials, again in a sentence or two.

The DICTION of the original is important. Name two or three key words or buzz words that need to be defined (in the researcher's terms) for the reader.

This could be another two or three sentences, written clearly and matching the researcher's point precisely.

FINDINGS need to be summarized. With complete sentences, mention key discoveries or insights of the study.

Scientific studies must have a SAMPLE SIZE, and you must identify who or what was studied, how many, and other statistical key points.

METHODOLOGY is the purpose of the study, the scientific process used to test the hypothesis, and you must tell what method was employed.

Most studies have RECOMMENDATIONS, if not SOLUTIONS, to what they have studied. Report in concise terms what may be the end result of the study, or what further study is indicated.

Once this information is culled from the original document, you are ready to write an abstract of 150 to 250 words.

APERçU

The French word for impression, an *Aperçu* does not attempt to analyze or to evaluate. It is a descriptive consideration at first glance. Its purpose is to give the reader sense of immediacy and presence at an event.

Most often, the *Aperçu* is used to depict sensory and transitory experience, something intangible and ephemeral. It is essentially descriptive. Metaphor or associated images are possible, but used sparingly. The purity of the experience is what is to be achieved.

In writing, the *Aperçu* is frequently used to evoke the actual experience of a sporting moment or event by using all the senses, which cannot be achieved through video or telecast.

THESIS: Describe an overall sensory impression.

DETAILS:
The five senses must be evoked to explain the uniqueness of the event. How are these senses illustrated?

SIGHT TOUCH SMELL HEARING TASTE

To develop fully your description, try to give a few graphic details to illustrate the five senses.

An *Aperçu* is a paragraph of at least 150 words. Keep your descriptive paragraph densely packed with sensory detail.

LITERARY DIGEST

Related to the abstract, but for creative projects, you may need to write a summary account. In this case you will do a digest is a brief explanation and condensed version of the larger document, story, or film. Using a sense of microcosm, the digests give a miniature version of the larger with a critic's eye. Most digests focus on storyline and plot, but can be used like abstracts.

Digests are short opinion and analytical works, no more than a few paragraphs. They can be general in tone and format, but they attempt to provide a reader with the flavor, mood, style, tone, image, and theme, of the larger.

Thesis: What is the apparent point of the project? Can you summarize the message or theme of the tale?

Name several dominant images or prefigures (power symbols) that epitomize the segment--and tell what they represent.

Prefigure what it represents:

a.
b.
c.
d.

How does the creative project create anticipation for the larger work?

a.
b.
c.

How are characters (or audience) challenged by the events?

a.
b.
c.

What rites or rituals (augurs) are used in the digest?

a.

b.

What unique, odd, or unusual details create a mood?

a.

b.

c.

What predictions can you make, based on the digest?

a.

b.

MINUTES OF A MEETING

One of the least thankful jobs is taking minutes at a meeting. Though you may be pressed into service, there are a few rules to bear in mind.

First, you need not copy every word said. In fact, it is preferable to summarize statements and not necessarily quote individuals unless they supply prepared remarks. In that case, you may make their contribution an attachment to the minutes.

Minutes are generally short, depending on the length of the meeting and the precedent of the business. Usually one or two pages is sufficient. Those who take minutes are not court stenographers who must take down every word.

The flavor or sense of the discussion or guest speakers may be given.

All minutes begin with the date of the meeting, its location, and the names of the attending individuals, especially if they have signed a sheet marking their presence. Usually members in attendance are listed alphabetically, though rank may figure into certain business situations.

Previous minutes are offered for approval and duly noted. It may be a good idea to circulate a draft of minutes before the next meeting to make sure there are no surprises at the meeting.

If elections are held, votes are reported and codified.

Remarks by dignitaries or officials are encapsulated with their names.

Headings such as Discussion may be used when an issue is raised.

If a motion is made, voted upon, and accepted or rejected, the minutes must reflect the exact wording of the motion as well as the exact vote of yea or nay.

Bold headings for different changes in the flow of the meeting may be helpful.

Minutes should also note the time of adjournment.

CONSPECTUS

Resembling a resume, a conspectus is a profile of an individual that highlights career or personal information, usually as a public relations vehicle.

These are popular as a thumbnail sketch with succinct data provided. The most famous example is the old-fashioned movie newsreel. Nowadays, a conspectus frequently becomes a personality profile used by management in company newsletters to announce new employees, etc.

If your assignment requires you to write a conspectus for your subject's life, for depiction in a company newsletter or blog, you would note the following:

Make a list of key information that must be woven into a paragraph.

PERSONAL DATA:

Name:
Nickname:
Hometown:
Education:
Hobbies:
Extra-curricular activities:
Awards/ citations/honors:
Most memorable lifetime moment:

DO THIS SECTION AS BULLETS (complete sentence list; items parallel please).

Segment must have an opening sentence and a closing sentence:

Notable Career Facts:

Achievements:

1.
2.
3.

Key Events in Career:

1.
2.

Personal Successes:
1.
2.
3.
3.

ROUTINE INQUIRY MEMORANDUM
(not an e-mail)

TO: Name or Title
FROM: Your Name, followed by your initialed signature
SUBJECT: Short Phrase, Initial Words Capped
DATE: Whatever style is appropriate to your company

Start with an INTRODUCTORY ¶.

Your opening is a modified hook/thesis. Ask in a general fashion for the information you require. Avoid a simple yes or no question. This section should be two or three sentences, approximately.

One middle BACKGROUND ¶ is recommended. Depending on the nature of your request, this section has two options. First, you may have sub-inquiries of the main subject. Second, you may need to provide a background to help the audience understand your inquiry. In either case I recommend a list from here; lists are quicker to read and understand. The audience will not be confused by complexity if listed step-by-step.

A third and CLOSING ¶ is essential. This short finish has several important purposes. First, it expresses goodwill and gratitude. Diplomacy is a key to success in business relationships. More important, this closing will provide any instructions, rules, or directions the audience requires to process and to respond to your inquiry.

****

Remember: if you use lists, paragraphing and spacing should be consistent.

1. All list points should be sentences or all phrases.

2. Lists have special indenting features.

3. Lists must end with the same punctuation, either periods or semicolons.

4. The last item ends with a period regardless of the punctuation.

Here is a helpful template:

ROUTINE INQUIRY OR RESPONSE STRATEGY is used in order to seek information or to answer a question is the most basic transactional writing process in business.

Dear ------(name or title):

SUBJECT: Number of Account or ID, or Short Phrase

INTRO ¶: THESIS OF YOUR ISSUE

KEY POINTS ¶ : Topic Sentence and list of answers, questions, or highlights.

Topic Sentence:

1.
2.
3.
4.
(ALL ITEMS MUST BE PARALLEL IN STRUCTURE)

 GOOD WILL CLOSE ¶:

PANEGYRIC

Another difficult strategy of public relations writing is to produce copy that lauds, compliments, or otherwise provides a positive portrait of an unpleasant or unlikeable figure or idea.

Your assignment may be to write a speech lauding one of the most repulsive and disliked people in your company. You must take the facts and put a rosy-colored spin on them.

You are now a spin-doctor! We recommend that you match up your candidate or idea to the Seven Cardinal Virtues (Faith, Hope, Charity, Justice, Courage, Prudence, and Moderation). Find an example or two for those qualities and match them in your writing.

Introduction:
Provide a Thesis that lauds your idea or person.

First Body Paragraph:
TOPIC SENTENCE: Explain all the virtues your subject shown or has developed. Start with your general opinion.

Use these details as part of the first body paragraph. A narrative paragraph serves the purpose and will prove preferable to a list, but for outline purposes, write a few ideas down before you begin to write.

VIRTUE:

WHAT QUALITY PROVES IT?

1.
2.

3.

4.

5.

6.

7.

Second Body Paragraph:

Discuss examples of positive compliments. You can have one or two examples for a virtue or two, or six examples for one virtue, depending on your topic. Make a quick list of possibilities before you begin to write a narrative paragraph.

1.

2.

3.

4.

5.

6.

7.

This paragraph should end with your topic sentence.

TECHNICAL WRITING ISSUE

Though you may never have to write a label, you should know what components go into writing directions or establishing a cautionary list.

Labels are essentially a variation on a pandect. They contain specific information in four general categories. Labels change according to the visual cues and marketing devices.

LABEL OUTLINE FORM

Your label should have four segments: Brainstorm and place details under appropriate headings.

DESCRIPTION: This section serves as a sales pitch, clarifying the purpose of the product and presenting its qualities in a positive manner.

1.
2.
3.
4.

DIRECTIONS: This section provides a step-by-step explanation on how to use the product.

1.
2.
3.
4.

CAUTIONS: This segment lists or explains the warnings or dangers of product abuse.

1.
2.
3.
4.

INGREDIENTS: This segment presents the various chemicals and inclusions in the product. It is done according to amount, largest first, and is a legal requirement of the government.

1.
2.
3.
4.

CLAIMS OR COMPLAINT LETTER

Month Day, Year

Audience Name
Street Address
City, State Zipcode

Dear (Always name or title):

SUBJECT:
Identify situation by Account Number, Reference Number, or
Order Number; use phrase if none of these is known.

INTRODUCTORY ¶

Your complaint or grievance is the thesis. State your problem
directly and unemotionally. Avoid an angry tone or hostile
attitude. The facts should speak for themselves; this section may
be a sentence or two.

BACKGROUND ¶

Start with a topic sentence. Then, explain the facts of your case.
You may also tell of the effects of the error or complaint. This
section is to gain sympathy to resolve your problem quickly.
Again, a diplomatic tone helps.

CORRECTIVE STEPS ¶
Start with a topic sentence that states you have several remedies.

1. I recommend a list on this section;
2. The audience can clearly see what must be done;
3. You may use commands or sentences for this list;
4. You are the injured party.

CLOSING ¶

This should be a close done in goodwill style. If the offense is serious, you may phrase your close into a warning about future business relationships.

Don't be too harsh. You do want to have the problem rectified effectively, not ignored or dismissed.

Yours sincerely,

Signed here

Your Typed Name

****NOTE: This form can be adapted to a memorandum for inter-office purposes.*

TEMPLATE FOR CLAIMS LETTER

SUBJECT LINE: (ID number or short description of problem)

INTRO ¶: (THESIS will sum up problem.)

BACKGROUND ¶:

Deductive Topic Sentence:

1.
2.
3.
4.
5.

RECOMMENDATIONS LIST:

Deductive Topic Sentence:

INDENTED LIST
1.
2.
3.
4.
(ALL ITEMS MUST BE PARALLEL STRUCTURE.)

GOODWILL CLOSING ¶:

1.
2.

THANK YOU STRATEGY FOR LETTER OR E-MAIL

Several reasons can be found for using this approach: first, to acknowledge donated time and service; second, to acknowledge a meal; third, to acknowledge a gift, no matter how small; or fourth, to acknowledge and to remind about your job interview.

Furthermore, this tactic may also work best when it does NOT seem obviously a routine thank you note. The value of this strategy is to build a relationship and encourage goodwill in an age when courtesy and politesse is becoming rare.

This strategy is best when you remember to apply a few rules:

1. Mention other people who were involved (i.e., a secretary, spouse, friends).

2. Say "thank you" only once in your letter.

3. Stay away from clichés and trite expressions that sound insincere or canned.

4. Do NOT sneak a request for another or second favor into your letter.

5. Add a personal handwritten postscript to any typed letter of thank you. Because this is nowadays in email format, you do not add emoticons, or create an artificial card with illustrations. Make your memo or letter simple and unadorned.

INTRODUCTORY ¶

Here you thank the person, mention what it is you are thankful for, and tell how pleased you are (about two sentences).

BODY ¶:

Explain why the gift is useful, or helpful, or why you appreciate the gesture extended to you (topic sentence and detail sentences).

Topic Sentence opens your paragraph:

1. You should provide narrative details, or points of an anecdote.

2. This ¶ should be long enough to indicate how meaningful you find the act.

3. Your special feeling for the audience ought to be stressed.

CLOSING ¶:

Express future wishes, hopes to reciprocate, or special goodwill (about two sentences at most).

DO NOT REPEAT YOUR THANK YOU EXPRESSION!

Sign off your letter or email with traditional closing.

INVITATION (e-mail or letter outline)

When you have an event, you may want to save on printed cards, and simply send out a pleasant notification. You can be creative and use different colors, fonts, backgrounds, and images, keeping the tone in synchronization with your organization and muted pleasantry.

INTRODUCTORY ¶. Begin with your Thesis.

What is the forum (exactly), and what can this invited guest contribute?

Another sentence is also advisable to express your appreciation overall for attending.

¶-- Give the audience the particulars such as time, place, and purpose. Answer as best you can.

1.
2.
3.
4.
5.
6.

¶-- How can guests contact you, deadlines, etc.? Bear in mind that for most people the acronym "RSVP" is not completely understood, and you may want to state the importance of letting you know whether a guest will attend (and with or without another).
1.
2.
3.
4.
5.

¶ -- Close is good will, stating directions, reminders, or other pertinent information.

1.
2.
3.

Sincerely,

COVER LETTER

Month Day, Year

Name of Prospective Employer
Address
City, State Zip code

Dear (Use a name or title):

SUBJECT: Official Job Title or HR Identification

AN INTRODUCTORY ¶ starts with a Thesis: state the job you are seeking.

Use the exact job title, and mention the code number, if applicable. Another sentence could explain how you learned of the position, or your objective in seeking the position.

REQUIREMENTS ¶

The job advertisement may list duties, responsibilities, or requirements. Match your qualifications to the job. You should explain how you best fulfill the job features. The paragraph length depends on your credentials. End the paragraph with a topic sentence that sums up your abilities: "As you can see, I am well-qualified for the position."

SPECIAL FEATURES ¶

Everyone has unique qualities that give a distinctive touch to what we do. In this paragraph you should stress your talents, those abilities not required, but that prove you are a valuable and impressive candidate for the job. This paragraph too ends with a topic sentence that sells you!

GOODWILL CLOSE ¶

Certain directions are stressed here: Are you available for an interview? Re-state your telephone number. There is no topic sentence in this paragraph, and it is quite short.

Respectfully yours,

Sign here

Your name typed

*****NOTE: Never photocopy a cover letter; write an original for each job.*

RULES FOR RESUMES

Everyone recommends a style for resumes. There is no correct form.

Whatever best represents you works. The key is to be consistent, neat, and to follow a few indisputable facts. A resume does not win a job for you.

Employers use resumes to screen their applicants. The resume will LOSE a job for you. The more you list on a resume, the more you provide that could disqualify you.

1. A resume should be an accurate picture of you at your present stage of life.

2. You need only one resume. If you want to stress different qualification for different jobs, do so in the cover letter.

3. You do NOT need an objective line. This too is an aspect of your cover letter. Career objectives may not apply to every job you send your resume.

4. Grammar, spelling, and punctuation, are main points of a resume. If you cannot proofread one page, you indicate that you cannot do any concentrated work. Who would hire an English major who doesn't capitalize English, or a management major who can't spell his subject?

5. There is no Personal Data section: age, height, weight, and marital status, et al, are illegal to ask. After you have the job, these facts will be provided for insurance reasons, affirmative action forms, etc. You never give your Social Security Number until the job is safely yours.

6. You do NOT need to list your hobbies. If the employer/interviewer inquires about these, it is usually to serve as an icebreaker to have you feel more comfortable.

7. Should your resume start with EDUCATION or EXPERIENCE?

This depends on you. If you are fresh out of school, your education is most important. If you have done work in your field, your experience ought to be stressed. List either category from most recent to the most distant.

8. Give only a short job description or title. Most titles are self-explanatory. If your job deserves special description, do that in the cover letter.

9. Be careful in listing religious and/or political affiliations. As unfair as it seems, some people may use these to disqualify you for the job. Keep your resume apolitical.

10. Be sure your social networking site, like Facebook, does not contradict your resume information. Also, be aware that many employers now routinely double-check facts with Facebook accounts.

Your resume is an evolving document. Keep it up to date.

PERSUASIVE SALES LETTER

Month Day, Year

Name of Audience
Street Address
City, State Zip code

Dear (Use Name):

INTRODUCTION ¶

Your first sentence in this paragraph is a hook. That is a thesis that grabs the reader's attention and arouses his interest, causing him to read on.

You may follow the hook with a short explanation of the comfort of the product.

DESCRIPTIVE ¶

Whether the product is a service or something concrete, you must describe what you are selling. Adjectives and words with positive connotations are needed. How big is it? What color is it? Or, how does it work? The product must be defined in glowing, but realistic terms. Your paragraph is inductive, leading the reader to accept your topic sentence.

REMOVING RESISTANCE or OBJECTIONS ¶

This is a difficult paragraph. You are not giving the buyer a reason to refuse. You put yourself in the buyer's place and suppose what he might say to reject you product. Then, you break down his sales resistance and objections by showing those reasons are not valid. If it's a question of cost, you may hint at the amount for that price--or that a sale price is now in effect.

Your paragraph ends with an inductive conclusion or topic sentence.

SPECIAL FEATURES OR BENEFITS ¶

Here is where you make your true sales pitch. In this paragraph you will cite details that differ from descriptive points. These are the unique or extraordinary features of the product or service. In some instances you may suggest examples and points that are strictly fringe benefits. You may note practical benefits of the product. It depends on what you are selling. You still end the paragraph with a topic sentence, which the reader should agree with.

GOODWILL CLOSE ¶

This short paragraph has no topic sentence. By now you assume the sale is made. You tell the buyer what he needs to know to purchase the product. You explain what he must do: is there a phone number to call? Is there a coupon to fill out?

Best wishes,

****NOTE: Absolutely no commands are used. You do not order customers or buyers. Your tone is polite and soft. Rhetorical questions are good sales devices.*

PERSUASIVE SALES OUTLINE and TEMPLATE:

You need a thesis to hook the audience:

I. ℐ Describe the Product.

1.
2.
3.
4.
5.
6.
7.
8.
End your paragraph with an INDUCTIVE TOPIC SENTENCE:

II. ℐ Removing Buyer Objections:

OBJECTION HOW TO REMOVE IT
1.
2.
3.
4.
End your paragraph with an INDUCTIVE TOPIC SENTENCE:

III. ℐ Special Features or Benefits Derived from Product or Idea:
1.
2.
3.
4.
5.
6.
End your paragraph with an INDUCTIVE TOPIC SENTENCE:

¶ DIRECTIONS: GOODWILL CLOSE HAS NO TOPIC SENTENCE

1.
2.
3.

BAD NEWS LETTER

Month Day, Year

Name of Audience
Street Address
City, State Zip code

Dear (use a name OR title):

INTRODUCTORY ¶

This paragraph buffers the audience with a thesis that is totally neutral about the crisis or situation. You may express sympathy, respect, or concern, but no sorrow is expressed unless it is absolutely warranted.

BACKGROUND ¶

You need a list of points both parties can agree upon. These points can be neutral, negative, or positive, or inconsequential. You are to lull the audience into a less volatile mood by illustrating the range of your sympathy and agreement. This paragraph is inductive.

BAD NEWS ¶

Here is where the bad news is delivered. You need about four sentences. You may structure the bad news from least to worst, or you can build with explanation to the bad news, placed in the last sentence of the paragraph. There is no topic sentence here; the worst news is the point.

NEUTRAL CLOSE ¶

This part is simply a good will close, hoping for a better future, etc. There is absolutely no reference whatever to the problem or situation that has been the source of bad news.

Cordially,

Signed here
Your Name

*****NOTE:*

The purpose of this strategy is to minimize bad feelings in an audience that is receiving news that he does not appreciate. The bad news is usually expected, but the tactic attempts dilute the strong emotion. Longer sentences are strongly advised; these require digestion and re-reading, thus the reader on an intellectual plane.

The most difficult part of this strategy is the rule: NO NEGATIVE WORDS CAN APPEAR IN THIS LETTER. To be successful, this letter must accentuate the positive. Forbidden words: no, not, never, don't, won't, can't, shouldn't, and the like; you should not use words with negative connotations, *i.e.,* 'allegations' or 'claims.' This tactic requires practice and ingenuity.

You may need to test your vocabulary to its limits in seeking neutral words.

BAD NEWS OUTLINE

THESIS: NEUTRAL OVERVIEW. BLAND. SYMPATHY. CONCERN. INTEREST. NO SORROW. NO APOLOGY.

BACKGROUND: (These points are agreeable to both sides, even if unfavorable.)

1.
2.
3.
4.
5.
6.
Topic Sentence:

BAD NEWS PARAGRAPH: (These points are unpleasant truths; absolutely no negatives can be used. Details are in order of bad to worst).

1.
2.
3.
4.
5. (Worst news)
YOUR WORST NEWS IS THE TOPIC SENTENCE.

CLOSE: (ABSOLUTELY NO REFERENCE TO PROBLEM OR BAD NEWS).
1.
2.
NO NEGATIVE WORDS CAN APPEAR ANYWHERE IN YOUR LETTER.

ANYTHING NEGATIVE CAN BE TURNED AROUND AND STATED POSITIVELY.

POLICY WRITING:
Short Memorandum Report

TO:
FROM:
SUBJECT:
DATE:

STATEMENT OF THE PROBLEM

Each section of the report has a titled heading. This section is also called the Executive Summary on occasion. Whatever it is called, it is an introductory paragraph. Your thesis and topic sentences derived from other sections comprised this opening. Though is comes first, it is often the last section to be written. Since memo reports are short by definition, this section is usually one paragraph, longer rarely.

FACTS OF CASE

This deductive paragraph is self-explanatory. This segment's length may be several paragraphs, depending on the complexity of the situation.

Objective and final, this section should clearly enumerate what is true, what is false, or what is known. No opinion or theory should be here.

ANALYSIS

This is often the most complex part of the report, and also the longest. Deductive and formal, this section takes the salient facts and evaluates them, considers ramifications, and digests these elements. Your options and theories are tested here. The quality of the analysis, however, will rest fully on your own insights and abilities to think.

RECOMMENDATIONS

After an opening topic sentence, this section may be in a list format.

• These items are strictly actions and directions based on analysis.

• Writers often put analysis in this section. It belongs elsewhere.

• The report is, by name, short: no more than several pages.

• Section headings, as seen above, are in caps and centered before each segment.

ANALYTICAL REPORT OUTLINE FORM

The Analytical Report is done in sections, with each segment headed by its title, in bold or underlined. Each ¶ features a deductive topic sentence.

EXECUTIVE SUMMARY

This section is your overview. As this is a lengthy report, this segment is several ¶s long on average. Your thesis and all topic ideas are covered here.

RESEARCHER BIAS

This segment details the prejudices, theories, or other assumptions under which the researcher or writer has conducted his study. This section provides insight into personal attitudes toward subject.

BACKGROUND OF PROBLEM

Facts about subjects should be: who, what, where, when, why.

This segment contains the substantive body of your report.

ANALYSIS

Another major segment: discussion, ramifications, and expectation results of problem. This details the reasons for your decisions, opinions.

RECOMMENDATIONS

Provide a list of match-ups.

PERSONNEL REPORT

TO:
FROM:
SUBJECT:
DATE:

EXECUTIVE SUMMARY ¶

This section is, in fact, an introductory paragraph. Headings are used. Thesis and topic sentence from other sections will comprise this opening.

METHODOLOGY ¶

This paragraph is deductive. Here you should explain what sources and methods (Statistics? History? *Etc*.) are used to compile this report on the individual. Items such as written work, transcripts, supervisor evaluation, *etc.*, should be cited.

POSITIVE POINTS ¶

This deductive paragraph will enumerate the examples of the employee's strong qualities. Concrete examples are useful and factual. As in all other sections, the writer should adopt a formal writing style, using no first-person pronouns, which could sound highly subjective.

NEGATIVE POINTS ¶

This paragraph is also deductive. You will enumerate here those points, which may not be favorable to the performance of the subject. Again, concrete examples, rather than opinions, will strengthen the quality of your work. Beware of making libelous statements.

RECOMMENDATIONS ¶

In some instances you will be required to pass judgment on the subject. Under these circumstances, you begin with a topic sentence and follow with a list of corrective actions, as company policy dictates.

. . . .

NOTE: Personnel Reports are usually confidential, but not always. You should be factual, therefore, in case the report is made available to the employee. All reports are best written in a formal, objective style--using no first person pronouns. All paragraphs are deductive. Although headings are often recommended, each paragraph should read as if it did not have a heading.

COLLECTIONS: REMINDER LETTER

Month Day, Year

Name of Audience
Street Address
City State Zip code

Dear (Use name):

INTRODUCTORY ¶

Your thesis for this first collection letter is a gentle statement about the
account. Often, a question is an effective way to start.

BODY ¶

The depth of the business relationship will have a bearing on the
collection series of letters. To begin, you give the audience an assumption of
innocence: hints at forgetfulness, computer snafus, clerical error, will soften
the notice. It also provides the client with a diplomatic excuse to remit his bill
late.

GOODWILL CLOSE¶
Here you stress the business friendship or association and look forward
to hearing from the client.
Yours,

Your name

*****NOTE:*

Often these first letters have the imprint of a form letter. Some strategists believe this lessons the hospitality or discomfort of the parties. Many companies also have several reminder letters used with care depending on the client and his importance.

ADDRESSING AN ENVELOPE

A forgotten art? A skill never taught? Young people seem never to have looked at an envelope on the outside. Isn't this task done automatically?

No, and with computerized address systems that frequently misspell, ignore commas, and other punctuation, the art of addressing an envelope may become a dim memory, a function performed automatically by an impersonal machine.

Birthday cards and holiday cards may be purchased, but an inability to make out the envelope may doom them to the Dead Letter Office at the Post Office unless some postal worker makes a valiant effort.

Your own address goes in the left-hand corner. With stickers and rubber stampers available, this can likely be avoided. Woe to you who buys an incorrectly written stamper.

Your name is at the top, with title in professional correspondence. Believe it or not, some young people will hold the envelope incorrectly and may try to align the envelope like a shopping list. The broadest side should face you.

Underneath is your street address. It should be spelled out, but usually is not. Avenue, Road, Street, Way, Lane, and other parts of the street address are in capital letters. Abbreviations often are indecipherable, from A to R to Ln, and all without a period ending the abbreviation. Spell it out, and worry not about punctuation.

The other major headache is the name of your city, the state, and zipcode. Cities' first letter are capitalized and followed by the state (first letter should be capped), but using Post Office abbreviations is best. TWO letters, no period. Consult the Post Office for your state's official postal abbreviation.

Most important of all is the name and address of the recipient. You want the message to arrive. Use a title: Mr. or Mrs., Ms or Miss, Master, Dr., Prof., Director, *etc*. Always be certain you have spelled the recipient's name correctly or given them the correct title.

Addresses, including city and state and zip, should follow the same rule as writing your own.

The process becomes sticky when there is an apartment, or other unusual address issue:

Prof. John Doe, Jr.
123 Main Street, Apt. 6
City, State 00000

You may have a business address:

Doe Medical Associates
123 Main Street, Suite 321
City, State 00000

ATTN: Dr. John Doe, Sr.

A Proofreading Checklist

Here are a few helpful hints to insure your writing is correct and clear:

APPEARANCE: You should take some pride in your personal work. Neatness not only counts, but it has its psychological values.

ADEQUATE CONTENT: Be sure that you have the sufficient number of paragraphs to make your strategy work effectively. Be certain that you cite adequate detail, spaced in its own sentence. Don't cram all of your details into one sentence.

INTRODUCTION: The first paragraph of every piece of business writing should have a thesis.

BODY PARAGRAPH: Check to be certain that inductive paragraphs have topic sentences at the end; deductive should have topic sentences at the start. Some memoranda have topic headings; letters do not.

SPELLING AND PUNCTUATION: Have a dictionary, thesaurus, and grammar book by your side, or use the tools on your computer program. Check anything of which you are uncertain.

FORMAT: Have you placed colons after the greeting of letters? Are there commas after each closing? Are headings consistent-- all caps are all underscored?

TRANSITIONS: Is there a logical sequence to the order of your detail? Commas are after all transitional words or expressions that start sentences?

RUN-ON SENTENCES, COMMA SPLICE SENTENCES, AND FRAGMENTS:
Nothing is more mortifying than a grievous grammatical flaw. Proofread each sentence from last to first, as units, examining all with a critical eye for overall content.

DICTION: The key to successful writing is in your verbs. Select strong, expressive verbs. Avoid clichés--or from using the verb 'get' or 'got' or 'gotten.'

HEADINGS: Reports have headings, usually in caps or underscored before each section. You may want to make your own personal list of specific errors. There are a dozen types of comma mistakes. Which error do you frequently make? Do you have items in a series? Did you add a comma before a "which" clause? Did you put a comma between two complete sentences? Make a note of it.

IN CLOSING: GENERAL POINTS

1. Make sure your sentences are complete subject/main verb combinations.

2, A sentence is a complete unit of thought.

3. Incomplete sentences are fragments that are rationally and grammatically incomplete.

4. All quoted material (even single words) is surrounded by quotation marks.

5. If you remove material from a quotation, replace it with an ellipsis.

6. Use the PRESENT tense consistently.

7. Do NOT address readers as "you" in general essays, only in journalism and business writing.

8. Assume your reader does not have access to background readings; provide the reader with the information he needs to understand.

9. Use your dictionary and thesaurus, or the program tools on your computer.

10. Quantity is not necessarily a virtue.

www.ingramcontent.com/pod-product-compliance
Lightning Source LLC
Chambersburg PA
CBHW081221170526
45165CB00009B/2905